YOU CAN DO IT !

Things You Can Do To MAKE YOUR CONGREGATION A CARING CHURCH

PAUL J CAIN

CONCORDIA PUBLISHING HOUSE · SAINT LOUIS

Ann,
I thank the Lord for you and how you care for me.

Humble yourselves, therefore, under the mighty hand of God so that at the proper time He may exalt you, casting all your anxieties on Him, because He cares for you. (1 Peter 5:6–7)

Copyright © 2013 Concordia Publishing House
3558 S. Jefferson Ave., St. Louis, MO 63118-3968
1-800-325-3040 · www.cph.org

All rights reserved. Unless specifically noted, no part of this publication may be reproduced, stored in a retrieval system, or transmitted, in any form or by any means, electronic, mechanical, photocopying, recording, or otherwise, without the prior written permission of Concordia Publishing House.

The quotations from the Lutheran Confessions are from *Concordia: The Lutheran Confessions*, second edition; edited by Paul McCain, et al., copyright © 2006 Concordia Publishing House. All rights reserved.

Scripture quotations are from the ESV Bible® (The Holy Bible, English Standard Version®), copyright © 2001 by Crossway Bibles, a publishing ministry of Good News Publishers. Used by permission. All rights reserved.

Catechism quotations are taken from *Luther's Small Catechism with Explanation*, copyright © 1986, 1991 Concordia Publishing House. All rights reserved.

Hymn texts with the abbreviation *LSB* are from *Lutheran Service Book*, copyright © 2006 Concordia Publishing House. All rights reserved.

1 2 3 4 5 6 7 8 9 10   22 21 20 19 18 17 16 15 14 13

TABLE OF CONTENTS

	Introduction	4
1	Understand Why You Care	6
2	Show Uncommon Common Sense	15
3	Care for the Community	35
4	Care for Church Workers and Their Families	52
5	Care for the Congregation	69
	Conclusion	93

A caring congregation? My Lutheran church?

My first real mentor in ministry was a retired pastor who taught our seventh-grade confirmation class during a vacancy. He taught us Luther's Evening Prayer as the closing prayer at the end of all of our Wednesday classes together. It was never part of our memory work, but we all had it memorized by the end of that year of instruction because we prayed it every week.

"Do your daily devotions" was another tip we heard each week. I always wanted to work up the courage to ask him, "How?" *Hymnal Supplement 98* and *Lutheran Service Book* taught me how to practically do that, with both full and simplified orders of daily prayer.

As a newly minted pastor and seminary graduate, I contacted a retired pastor mentor for advice on starting my first call. It was simple, yet profound: "Love your people."

His answer came in a now old-fashioned handwritten letter sent through the mail. I couldn't immediately ask him my question, "How?" In our subsequent correspondence, an answer became clear.

Love your people with the Word of Christ in all of its truth and all of its purity and with the Sacraments administered according to His institution and mandate. The seminary was a great blessing to us as we learned this pure doctrine, faithful practice, and to not take either for granted.

Fieldwork, vicarage, and those early days in the parish teach you the importance of both patience and tact. And how important it always is to love your people by getting to know them, sharing who you are, and by going the extra mile to give them truly Christian pastoral care. It is amazing what people will forgive if they know that you love them.

This book, *Five Things You Can Do to Make Your Congregation a Caring Church*, offers some additional insights, practical ones, into how to love your people. I pray it will be beneficial to you and to all you serve according to your God-given vocations, whether you are a pastor or the member of a Lutheran congregation.

One of the great blessings of The Lutheran Church—Missouri Synod has been a historic dual focus: keeping the message straight and getting the message out. The early history of the Synod (and much of its prehistory) shows a concern for both. During the great immigration periods when Germans found a new home in a new land, particularly the late nineteenth century and early twentieth century, members of the LCMS were there with a job, a place to stay, and a place to worship. God bless you as you provide those same caring actions today.

1

UNDERSTAND WHY YOU CARE

We love because He first loved us. (1 John 4:19)

[Jesus said,] "I am the good shepherd.
The good shepherd lays down His life for the sheep."
(John 10:11)

As Christians, we should care whether or not our congregations care about other people. We should also care how well that comes across. Imagine showing up at a friend's home one evening because you received an invitation to dinner. You walk up to the door a couple of minutes early and ring the doorbell. You wait. You ring it again and wait some more. Finally, your friend's wife answers the door. "Have a seat. There are magazines to look at while you wait for dinner." She isn't exactly rude, but she isn't friendly either.

As you wait, your friend's son walks by. He doesn't say a word. He doesn't even acknowledge your presence. Your friend's daughter, oblivious to her surroundings because of her MP3 music player, comes in the living room, slumps on the sofa, and zones out.

If you were this dinner guest, what would you think? How would you feel? What would you say?

Perhaps you've had an experience like this at a Christian congregation. As a one-time vacation visitor, I remember walking in to a congregation that had "LCMS" on the sign. I was greeted with a nod from someone who gave out the bulletins and spoke briefly with the pastor to announce for Communion, but I had little contact with anyone else in the congregation. No hellos. No handshakes. It was awkward at best. I was thankful that at least I wasn't "greeted" by someone like Grandma Schmidtke, who would've said, "You're sitting in my pew!"

We should care about those who walk in the doors of the Lord's house on the Lord's Day. We should care primarily because Jesus cared for us first. As the apostle writes, "We love because He first loved us" (1 John 4:19).

Jesus Cared during His Earthly Ministry

We should care today because our Lord cared for others during His earthly ministry. Jesus reads and preaches upon Isaiah 61, Jesus' own "call document" in Luke 4:18–21:

> "The Spirit of the Lord is upon Me, because He has anointed Me to proclaim good news to the poor. He has sent Me to proclaim liberty to the captives and recovering of sight to the blind, to set at liberty those who are oppressed, to proclaim the year of the Lord's favor."
>
> And He rolled up the scroll and gave it back to the attendant and sat down. And the eyes of all in the synagogue were fixed on Him. And He began to say to them, "Today this Scripture has been fulfilled in your hearing."

Who wants to hang out with the poor? Jesus does. He proclaims the Gospel to them. Jesus proclaims true freedom to captives and the oppressed. He delivers sight to those formerly blind. He announces that in Him, now is the time of salvation and the Lord's favor. Jesus cared for those He was given to care for.

Some wondered if Jesus was "the One." Jesus quickly answers the question delivered by the disciples of John the Baptist in Matthew 11:3–6:

> "Are You the one who is to come, or shall we look for another?" And Jesus answered them, "Go and tell John what you hear and see: the blind receive their sight and the lame walk, lepers are cleansed and the deaf hear, and the dead are raised up, and the poor have good news preached to them. And blessed is the one who is not offended by Me."

Jesus preaches, teaches, heals, and resurrects the dead in order to care for those He was sent to save. We should care for others because Jesus *still* cares for others like we once were. He still cares for people like we are now.

Jesus Still Cares for Us in Word and Sacrament at the Divine Service

Where does God in Christ primarily care for the people He calls together? The Divine Service! Jesus cares for us at church, where the Lord Himself regularly gathers to Himself a people to whom He distributes His good gifts!

Our German fathers and mothers in the faith called the service of Word and Sacrament *Gottesdienst*, "Divine Service" in English, specifically understood as "God's service to us."

In the twentieth century, it became trendy to speak of liturgy as "the work of the people." Not only is this historically and linguistically untrue, it is theologically inaccurate.

The title of "Divine Service" keeps our focus as Christians at worship on Christ and not ourselves. It reminds us that what primarily happens on Sunday mornings (and other times) is the Lord's work for us, rather than our work for God.

"Divine Service" communicates God's work for us in delivering His gifts to us more clearly than the titles "the Order of Morning Service," "the Eucharist," or "the Holy Communion."

"Divine Service" has the same focus as some other terms for the second part of a service of Word and Sacrament, such as "the Lord's Supper" or "the Lord's Table." It's important to remember that this isn't our Supper, but His.

Ask a Lutheran if we are saved by our works or saved by Jesus, and you will likely hear the biblical answer: by grace, through faith, in Christ alone. Amen!

Why, then, do a majority of Christians (American Evangelicals, Roman Catholics, the Eastern Orthodox, Mainline Protestants, Pentecostals, etc.) put so much focus on what *we* do on Sunday mornings instead of acknowledging a truly Christian and Lutheran theology of worship?

To be sure, we are given to return gifts to the Lord, pray,

praise, and give thanks. All of those actions of heart, mind, and body are our actions of response to the Gospel, the gift of the forgiveness of sins in Christ alone. At worship, the primary focus must remain on our triune God, both who He is and what He has done and still does for us.

Truly Christian worship focuses on Christ, not the Christian. The cross is where the forgiveness of sins was won. That forgiveness, life, and salvation, Jesus' care for us, is delivered in Word and Sacrament because God has promised to deliver His gifts through these means.

In the Lutheran Divine Service, the Lord shows He cares for you by delivering His gifts to you. In short, that is why we go to church, or more accurately, why the Lord gathers His people around these gifts.

In the Name

The Divine Service is begun by invoking God's revealed name. We call upon Him to be present with us. And His name, placed on us at Holy Baptism, recalls the promises He made to deliver His salvation to us in Holy Baptism. You may wish to skim through Divine Service III (*LSB*, pp. 184–202) as you read this chapter.

We are invited to confess our sins and confess that we are poor, miserable sinners, the "poor in spirit" of the Beatitudes (Matthew 5). Christ's care for us today, here and now, is announced by the Lord's servant: "Upon this your confession, I, by virtue of my office, as a called and ordained servant of the Word, announce the grace of God unto all of you, and in the stead and by the command of my Lord Jesus Christ I forgive you all your sins in the name of the Father and of the Son and of the Holy Spirit" (*LSB*, p. 185).

As God's Divine Service of us continues, the people gathered by the Lord hear His Word prayed, read, sung, and preached. Another blessing commonly concludes the pastor's sermon: "The peace of God, which passes all understanding, keep your hearts and minds in Christ Jesus" (*LSB*, p. 192).

As a portion of what the Lord has given us is returned to Him, we, with David, ask for more from Him in the Offertory. And as the Service of the Word portion culminated in the very words of Jesus, the Holy Gospel, so does the Service of the Sacrament. Note the blessings Jesus promises and delivers to care for you (*LSB*, p. 197).

> Our Lord Jesus Christ, on the night when He was betrayed, took bread, and when He had given thanks, He broke it and gave it to the disciples and said: "Take, eat; this is My body, which is given for you. This do in remembrance of Me."
>
> In the same way also He took the cup after supper, and when He had given thanks, He gave it to them, saying: "Drink of it, all of you; this cup is the new testament in My blood, which is shed for you for the forgiveness of sins. This do, as often as you drink it, in remembrance of Me."

UNDERSTAND WHY YOU CARE

The Lord's care for you continues as we prepare to depart. We pray with Simeon:

"Lord, now lettest Thou Thy servant depart in peace according to Thy word, for mine eyes have seen Thy salvation, which Thou hast prepared before the face of all people, a light to lighten the Gentiles and the glory of Thy people Israel. Glory be to the Father and to the Son and to the Holy Ghost; as it was in the beginning, is now, and ever shall be, world without end. Amen." (*LSB*, pp. 199–200)

The Lord's care for us should be reflected in our care for others. Consider our request for that very thing to happen in one of the historic prayers at the end of Divine Service:

We give thanks to You, almighty God, that You have refreshed us through this salutary gift, and we implore You that of Your mercy You would strengthen us through the same in faith toward You and in fervent love toward one another; through Jesus Christ, Your Son, our Lord, who lives and reigns with You and the Holy Spirit, one God, now and forever. (*LSB*, p. 201)

Amen to that!

What Gifts Does Jesus Give to Us?

The Second Article of the Apostles' Creed speaks of our redemption. We confess with Dr. Luther: "[He] has redeemed me, a lost and condemned person, purchased and won me from all sins, from death, and from the power of the devil . . . that I may be His own and live under Him in His kingdom and serve Him in everlasting righteousness, innocence, and blessedness" (Small Catechism).

Because we already care about other people, we want them to have all of these gifts.

The Lord delivers these gifts by the work of God the Holy Spirit through the means He has connected to His Bible promises. "The Holy Spirit has called me by the Gospel, enlightened me with His gifts, sanctified and kept me in the true faith. In the same way He calls, gathers, enlightens, and sanctifies the whole Christian church on earth" (Small Catechism, Third Article). It is easier to talk to people you already know about the weather, congregation business, or the win/loss record of a college football team than spiritual matters, but if we really and truly care about others and where they will spend eternity, we should care enough to tell others the Good News about Jesus and invite them to church.

A caring congregation has eyes for those who are alone, those who are new, and also for those who haven't been in church in a long time. You'll hear more about that in chapter 2.

Key Points

- Jesus cared for others during His earthly ministry.
- You care because He first cared for you.
- Jesus still cares for you at the Divine Service in Word and Sacrament.

Discussion Questions

1. Why might someone not care as much about being friendly or caring at church?
2. Many older Christians are hard-of-hearing. How can we care for them? How can we help them meet (and hear) new members and visitors?
3. Do you have friends, family, neighbors, or co-workers who do not attend a Christian congregation? Have you ever invited them to come with you? What obstacles might a visitor confront at your congregation?

Action Items

1. Review a proper Christian theology of worship by reading Dr. Norman Nagel's introduction to the 1982 LCMS hymnal, *Lutheran Worship* (pp. 6–7), as well as the theological introductions to both *Hymnal Supplement 98* (pp. 4–5) and *Lutheran Service Book* (pp. viii–ix).
2. Ask newer members of your congregation what it was like for them to visit for the first time. Did they have any unpleasant or unfriendly interactions? Listen patiently and carefully and act on their constructive criticism.
3. Make an intentional effort to speak to people at church in addition to your family and close friends. Look and pray for such an opportunity each Sunday.

2

SHOW UNCOMMON COMMON SENSE

I believe in God, the Father Almighty, maker of heaven and earth.

What does this mean? I believe that God has made me and all creatures; that He has given me my body and soul, eyes, ears, and all my members, my reason and all my senses, and still takes care of them. (Small Catechism, First Article)

If I've learned anything from those around me, it is a pithy new aphorism: "Common sense really isn't that common."

It's easy to get used to the way things are at church and not show any thought for why they are that way or if there is any need to improve them. This is not to say that everything is wrong or that change should be made for change's sake, but when it comes to our physical environment—which includes the people there—there are many items worth reviewing. Remembering that it is caring to notice and improve such things for the benefit of our eyes, ears, and other senses, let's discuss these common challenges in an uncommon yet Lutheran way. Moving from the outside in, we'll start with what people notice first.

Change is a scary word. But we are not discussing an alteration of Lutheran practices or teachings. Since physical setting frames what happens in the service, we want that frame to direct us to the gifts of the Divine Service, not distract from it. You wouldn't put a frame of rusty metal or pink neon around the Mona Lisa. Don't frame your church service that way either.

Parking

The larger and more urban your congregation is, the larger an issue parking tends to be. It may not be much of a problem for some smaller congregations. Even so, there are always challenges.

Know and clearly communicate where your members should and shouldn't park. Can people park on the street, in the lot next door, or on the grass? Do the owners of the business across the street mind if your members take the spots right in front of their doors? Being good neighbors is part of your congregation's witness to the community. Respect their property and needs as well as your own.

Rain and snow can be safety issues for your parking lot. Gravel, mud, and high heels do not mix well. Paving and sloping a church parking lot are good ideas to consider. Installing parking blocks or painting yellow parking spot lines can help too.

Consider parking spots for those with state handicap parking permits. Have special, convenient parking reserved near the front door for visitors, pregnant mothers, or families with small children.

Don't forget to note if there's a disconnect between the seating capacity of your church and room to park outside. If needed, look for ways to expand parking or to accommodate a larger-than-normal parking crowd for heavily attended services (such as the kid's Christmas program). As with other areas, plan ahead for the future needs of your congregation.

Your Church Building

"You only have one chance to make a first impression." At least once a year, put yourself in a visitor's shoes.

Are there weeds growing up in the cracks of the sidewalk leading to the church door? Is the church sign well-maintained and regularly lit? Has the lawn been mowed? Is everything you can see clean and in good repair?

Internally, is the carpet stained and the paint peeling? Are the paraments faded and unraveling? There are so many questions to ask.

We know that people *should* choose a church on the basis of what is believed, taught, and confessed. That said, not everybody chooses a congregation for all the right reasons. Work with your trustees to remove potential stumbling blocks with regard to your church facility. Also, keep in mind that this is the Lord's house. While we should not spend foolishly and extravagantly, God deserves our best. Even the simplest church should look like a holy dwelling, well-maintained as our place to meet Him face-to-face.

Try asking yourself the questions above (and more like them) on a typical Sunday morning, and do a similar survey of your church property on a weekday. Brainstorm a list of items to repair or replace. Prioritize safety issues. Perhaps you'll develop possibilities to use some memorial funds!

We care for all that the Lord has entrusted to us, including all church property, for the sake of the Gospel that we share with the people we are given to care.

Greeters

The people in your church, especially those serving in formal roles, are a crucial part of creating a caring environment. Greeters can be helpful, but not everyone has the temperament to be a greeter. Training can equip willing, living, breathing servants to be better at welcoming the Lord's people on the Lord's Day.

Often, unofficial greeters are already active in your congregation. Their faithful response to the Gospel of Jesus Christ is to look for others to care for in Jesus' name. Identify these people and encourage them to continue, officially or unofficially.

Greeters can introduce visitors and guests to the ushers, elders, and the pastor. This is helpful to pastoral care and administration of the Sacrament of the Altar as a faithful expression of our church body's Communion fellowship.

If you do not yet have official greeters for each service, consider recruiting a group of friendly greeters to care for visitors and members on Sunday morning.

"Sitters"

Allow me to offer an uncommon and perhaps more helpful alternative: sitters.

Consider having a handful of winsome and welcoming members who wait to find a seat in a pew.

Why? Some who attend worship may be alone on a Sunday morning, may be visiting for the first time, or may already be members but haven't been to a service in a while. Sitters could help your congregation care for visitors and members by sitting with them and answering basic questions about restrooms, baby changing tables, how to use the hymnal, and other issues.

Ushers

The role of an usher is not merely to pass out bulletins, collect the offering, or usher people out at the end of worship. Ushers may be the closest thing to greeters that a smaller congregation has.

An usher is often the first person a visitor asks about receiving the Lord's Supper. Train ushers to work with your Sunday elders on duty and your pastor so they aren't caught off-guard by such important questions. Pastors and elders will do well to alert ushers about visitors who are communing before they are put on the spot when it is time for a given pew to go up to receive the Sacrament.

Ushers, like elders, serve as an extension of the pastoral office. Annual training will help your ushers provide consistent and competent service to the pastor and congregation at worship.

Elders

Lay elders in a congregation are honored in their service to their Lord with a term used for the Office of the Holy Ministry in the New Testament. In very small congregations, a single elder on duty on a given Sunday may be a congregation's only greeter or usher, may come in early to unlock the doors, turn on the heat/air and lights, set up for Holy Communion, and serve as one of the offering counters. I thank the Lord for such selfless, dedicated, and often unsung heroes of the faith.

My elders have been available to meet and greet visitors from sister LCMS congregations at the last minute before the Divine Service while I'm vesting and sending the acolyte out to light candles. I sincerely appreciate their help in welcoming Christians from other LCMS congregations to the Lord's Table and asking other visitors to refrain from communing.

The LCMS's faithful, biblical, apostolic, confessional, and loving practice of closed Communion deserves at least a brief note here.

It is not loving or caring to invite a guest to partake of something that may be harmful to them because they have not examined themselves, are not repentant, do not discern the Lord's body, do not hold a biblical confession in harmony with the Scriptures and the Small Catechism, or do not know what the Lord's Supper is.

A five-minute conversation with a non-LCMS visitor is not enough time to do justice to the biblical doctrine of the Lord's Supper or to be truly caring to that visitor, your congregation, or our fellowship of pastors and congregations walking together in teaching and practice. Five minutes *may* be enough time to explain how we differ in Bible teaching and practice: why the ELCA and LCMS are not in fellowship, how Lutherans and Baptists differ on what the Bible teaches about Holy Baptism, or the simple truth that Roman Catholics and the Eastern Orthodox (among many others) practice closed Communion too.

Pastor, elders, ushers, greeters, and sitters are all on the same team, friendly helpers given to care for visitors and members in the pew.

Seating

Now that the people have parked, glanced at the building, and been greeted and ushered in, physical concerns once more arise. This starts with a question: how comfortable are your pews or sanctuary chairs? A congregation I served took a big step by purchasing padding for their pews for the first time. It was a challenge to make them comfortable enough to last through a service, yet not so comfortable that husbands dozed off during the sermon!

Like everything else, pews need to be maintained. Use oil soap for wood, and consider refinishing after decades of service. Padding takes special care because stains *will* happen. Candles will drip wax on Christmas Eve while you sing "Silent Night." My current congregation is blessed with the same pews since the "new" church was dedicated in 1958. Because repairs and proper cleaning have been done over the years, our artificial leather has held up well, and we're keeping a watch on springs and padding that may need to be replaced in the next few years.

Many churches also have kneelers. The pads, brackets, "feet," and other parts should be in good repair and well-oiled to avoid squeaks during prayers.

For some churches, the portability of chairs is appealing and gives a great deal of flexibility. Folding chairs are often necessary for mission congregations or for established congregations on Christmas and Easter. Comfort, cleaning, and durability should be carefully considered when chairs are used. Hard metal folding chairs may not be the best solution for the long-term. As with everything inside your sanctuary, consider new materials carefully. Do what it takes to care for or replace what you currently have.

Lighting and Sound

Having good lighting for worship really should be "common sense," but it has not always been so in my limited experience. Direct light works better than reflected light. Natural window light may not be enough or may not be possible due to stained glass or an interior room worship space. Also consider whether adjustable lighting would be of benefit to your congregation.

If your members or visitors find it hard to see the bulletin or hymnal on Sunday morning, your Voters Assembly will likely find it easy to pass a motion using memorial funds for better lighting!

Since church is all about hearing the Word of God, sound and sound systems can be very important. When I arrived at my current congregation, we were known as "Rice Krispies Lutheran Church" because our sound system seemed to "snap, crackle, and pop." It still took some time before the voters adopted a resolution upgrading the sound system.

Our former sound system had been pieced together over the decades. Original speakers from the old (pre-1957) building were brought over to be reused. Equipment used to broadcast services over live radio from the 1970s through the 1990s was housed in a 1960s tower originally designed for a now-defunct electronic church bell. Our 1980s wireless microphone system had to be replaced because of the way the federal government redistributed the broadcasting spectrum—it just wasn't reverent for emergency radio messages to come over our loudspeakers during church.

Our trustees put out for bids. A gifted local sound tech gave us a bid of under $7,000. That is still a lot of money, but it was far less than the $60,000 to $80,000 spent by other congregations in our town.

How were we able to get such a low bid? The trustees and I volunteered to help with the installation. We reused components from three unconnected sound systems already in the building. We focused most of our funds on good wired and wireless microphones, a new soundboard, new wiring, and new drivers for our decades-old speakers.

Since that initial investment, we have upgraded speakers in both our parish hall and "cry room" as overflow seating, bought a larger soundboard, incorporated microphones for our pianos, and found a simple way to record our services and continue to provide low-power FM radio hearing assistance to members. We've spent less than $2,000 more since that bid of $7,000.

We cared for our congregation by upgrading our sound system so our own members and our visitors could hear God's Word.

My first congregation didn't need a sound system. We had an intimately sized nave. We didn't record services for shut-ins since I could personally visit every shut-in in the congregation at least twice a month. This is to say that you should determine any possible investment in sound equipment based on the needs that have been determined and agreed upon. The needs of your congregation could be nothing, a few new wireless microphones, an overhaul of your soundboard, or a system of top quality broadcasting equipment.

My current congregation uses a digital recorder tied into the sound system to record every service (and Bible study). We use a free software program to edit services. We import the files into iTunes and burn CDs that go out to our shut-ins to play on donated CD-players. We even use permanent markers to color code the buttons on the CD-players to help our shut-ins transition to the "newer" technology: the PLAY button is colored green and the STOP button is red.

Whether you need a sound system, hearing assistance equipment, or a CD ministry to shut-ins or not, sound in your church on Sunday morning is important.

> How then will they call on Him in whom they have not believed? And how are they to believe in Him of whom they have never heard? And how are

they to hear without someone preaching? ...
So faith comes from hearing, and hearing
through the word of Christ. (Romans 10:14, 17)

LUTHERAN SERVICE BOOK:
A USER-FRIENDLY HYMNAL

No, it is not common to talk about hymnals alongside parking, lighting, sound, and friendliness, but we need to. Having quality, user-friendly hymnals is an important way a congregation shows it cares. Our 2006 LCMS hymnal, *Lutheran Service Book* (*LSB*), is indeed a user-friendly hymnal.

This hymnal is much easier for Lutherans and our visitors to use than its two predecessors. For all of the blessing that *The Lutheran Hymnal* (*TLH*) was and still is, it provided challenges to members and visitors alike. Fonts were relatively small and often difficult to read. *TLH* has a page 23 (in the middle of the "page 15" Service of Holy Communion"), Psalm 23 (in very small print on p. 128), and a hymn with the number 23, "Hallelujah! Let Praises Ring." *Lutheran Worship* (*LW*), our 1982 LCMS revision of *Lutheran Book of Worship* (*LBW*), did not improve on these weaknesses.

Will you bear with me for a "When I was on vicarage" story? As vicar, I was responsible for catechizing sixth and seventh graders. The vacancy pastor was to care for the eighth graders from his congregation and ours. To my knowledge, some of the families of the young people being confirmed that day had not been regular church attendees.

How does this fit into my hymnal story? When the vacancy pastor invited the congregation to "turn to page 158 for Divine Service II," in the front of *Lutheran Worship*, about half of the *confirmands* turned to hymn 158, "Come, Holy Ghost, Our Souls Inspire," in the middle of *LW*. I was embarrassed for them. There had to be a better way of organizing a hymnal!

Part of the untold, uncommon-sense story of the Lutheran Hymnal Project that led to *LSB* is the "radical" idea of ordering a hymnal based on Colossians 3:16: "Let the word of Christ dwell in you richly, teaching and admonishing one another in all wisdom, singing psalms and hymns and spiritual songs, with thankfulness in your hearts to God."

A brief tour of *LSB* should be sufficient, because it has only one numbering system.

A cross is most prominent on the front cover, surrounded by eight squares, representing Easter, the Resurrection of Our Lord as an eighth day of creation, as well as the expanding kingdom of Christ. The Means of Grace are displayed to the left, God's Word, Holy Baptism, and Holy Communion.

Prayers are found inside the front cover. Introductory material and lectionary resources are found on pages with Roman numerals.

In the Psalter of *LSB*, there are no page numbers other than psalm numbers. In *LSB*, number 1 is reserved for Psalm 1. The only number 23 is Psalm 23—there is no hymn 23 or page 23. Not every psalm is included in the pew edition, but numbers through 150 are reserved for the psalms alone. (Check the *LSB Altar Book* and electronic edition for all 150 psalms.)

Liturgies begin on page 151. One will find orders of service familiar from *The Lutheran Hymnal*, *Lutheran Worship*, and *Hymnal Supplement 98*. For the first time in an LCMS hymnal, orders for wedding and funeral are included in the pew edition. Luther's Small Catechism concludes this section on pages 321–30.

Hymns run from number 331 to 966 (with additional hymns and resources available in the electronic and musician editions).

The inside back cover has some commonly used texts for prayer, including the Nicene Creed, Apostles' Creed, and two translations of the Lord's Prayer. The back cover provides devotional art for Father, Son, and Holy Spirit. Because of the imprinted art, even Lutherans can "feel the Spirit." Overall, the size of *LSB* is similar to that of *LW* and *LBW*, yet it is significantly lighter than the weight of the initial printings of those hymnals and has larger print than *TLH*. Due to the color of the paper, it is easier to read in low light.

LSB is user-friendly because it is more than a printed book. Congregations that wish to print out hymns and liturgies may do so with *Lutheran Service Builder*. *Lutheran Service Builder* can provide PowerPoint slides for projection. Congregations that use the *LSB* family of resources finally have a faithful and user-friendly Lutheran hymnal that means one and only one thing by "turn to number 23": "The Lord is my shepherd. . . ." This was very caring of the Commission on Worship to do for us, our congregations, and our visitors.

Developing a User-Friendly Bulletin

Bulletins have grown in complexity from typewritten, mimeographed lists of hymns and liturgies to the mini-book modern marvels of desktop publishing.

It may be fun to play with the hundreds and thousands of available fonts, but I recommend sticking with those that are easy to read. Consider serif fonts like Times Roman, Garamond, Palatino, or Goudy Old Style. Sans serif fonts like Calibri, Segoe UI, and Trebuchet have gained common use. You may also wish to use the same fonts for your bulletin as you see in the hymnal.

Consider a font in a readable size. The smallest I would ever use is a 9-point font. When we have a funeral, we print out the entire service using *Lutheran Service Builder*. I resize congregational responses and Bible readings to at least 12-point. Page numbers are made 16-point. Our bulletins tend to stay around 11-point. We have made large-print bulletins available according to need.

Many congregations use a folded letter-size bulletin. Readings may be on the back or on a half-letter-size insert. Concordia Publishing House also has legal-sized bulletins available with the same three-year readings on the back. They could be folded in half. We fold them so that they look like the common letter-size bulletin, but with a three-inch-wide tab to the left. Readings are on the back. Announcements are inside. We print our entire service outline on the three-inch tab.

The tab bulletin and *Lutheran Service Book* work well together. Tuck the bulletin inside the back cover so that the tab sticks out. Any worshiper can see the whole service at a glance, whether the hymnal is open or closed. Your free hand could be used to pass the offering plate, hold a child, shake a hand, or elbow a sleeping family member.

Friendliness

I dearly love Grandma Schmidtke. Every congregation has someone like her. But it's hard not to take her greeting, "You're sitting in my pew," in a bad way.

The idea of "my pew" has a history. Even in Luther's day, there were no pews or seating in church naves. Here in America, back in the day, some wealthier congregation members may well have donated or paid for the actual pew their family sat in. I've even seen LCMS congregations where a particular family paid to have heating added for their family pew.

A more encouraging version of this story was a small congregation that was in a dual parish agreement with my home congregation for over fifty years. It was common for all twenty-six members to be in church most Sundays. Members left their personal hymnals in their pews. Since members here were so thrilled to have any visitor, guests were greeted with words like "Welcome. We're glad to have you join us for worship. Why don't you sit with my family in our pew?"

If you happen to receive unsettling words by someone, please don't take it personally. Don't judge the whole congregation based on one person's tactlessness. If you chance to overhear such words spoken to someone near you, offer a welcoming place to sit near you and your family.

Families with young (and sometimes crying) children don't deserve glares. Offer them help. Thank them for bringing the baptized—and unbaptized—children with them to church. And encourage them to come each week. As a matter of habit, If there are people you see at church that you haven't met, introduce yourself, or at least greet them with a pleasant "Hello." It never hurts to smile.

"Would all the visitors today please stand up and embarrass themselves?" Perhaps you haven't heard such an invitation at the end of a church service, but this is often how some visitors *hear* such announcements. Welcoming your guests is good; putting them on the spot is not.

As for new members, sometimes, instead of a formal liturgical introduction during a service after a family transfers in, some prefer to be welcomed with an announcement in that week's bulletin, a note in the next monthly newsletter, and a new photo in the church directory/membership photo wall.

Don't forget about greeting longstanding members too. "We've missed you" are among the most appropriate and caring words we can share with congregation members we haven't seen in a while, whether we catch a glimpse of them at the store or on a Sunday morning. But don't say it as a guilt trip. Show you genuinely care. Ask about what's going on in their lives. If there has been a major loss (death, layoff, family crisis, etc.), it may to be best to lead off with specific questions about such things. Share the love of Jesus. Say, "I'll pray for you." You could even offer to pray with them right then and there. Don't think this only applies to those who've been absent either. The people across the pew from you every Sunday also need your care and concern. Sincere greetings and interest in them personally is key to becoming a closer, stronger congregational community.

Expanding Sunday Morning

Our congregation keeps up a low-maintenance blog with basic contact information, service times, announcements, and sermons. If you have a Web site, make it easy to navigate. Fill it with helpful information. Make it more than a brochure. Keep it updated. Nobody likes "cobWeb pages," and they certainly don't reflect well on your congregation.

Consider offering Holy Communion at least once a Sunday. This is a good idea on its own merits and is of specific comfort to college students and shift workers. We have considered adding an 8 a.m. service to more comfortably accommodate our members on Sunday morning. In addition, we have thought of having Matins at 8 and Divine Service at 10:30 one week with Divine Service at 8 and Matins at 10:30 the next Sunday. Among the other possibilities your church might consider is adding an evening service on Saturday or Wednesday to meet the needs of frequent travelers and weekend workers.

With any of these changes, you may wish to recruit more elders, altar guild members, and musicians beforehand.

Stewards

As Christians, we are to be good stewards of the money, time, and talents the Lord has given. I pray you may also be reminded of our important vocation as stewards of His Gospel and His people. You've heard it said that "You can't take it with you." That's true, but only to a point. We can take the Lord's love and Word with us, for the Word of the Lord endures forever. And we will also be blessed to spend eternity with our Lord Jesus and all who have died in the faith.

Before church, pray for those who may hear the Gospel for the first time that the Holy Spirit may grant them faith. Pray for those in whom the seed of faith is starting to sprout that they may grow in that faith. Pray also for the blessed ones in whom faith has flourished that they may be kept strong in Christ as they share their faith with others.

A Sunday morning service is the most common time a congregation interacts with larger numbers of visitors. I pray that this chapter will help you welcome visitors in Jesus' name with His Word and His love. Our next chapter helps us see opportunities for Gospel outreach and human care in the community around your congregation.

Key Points

- While pure teaching and proper administration of the Sacraments are the highest priorities, parking, seating, lighting, and sound are also of importance.

- You care for members and visitors with a user-friendly hymnal and by having a bulletin that is helpful and easy to read.
- Focusing on people is key. Equip elders, greeters, "sitters," ushers, and other members to provide friendly help in the pew.

Discussion Questions

1. Can your congregation accommodate members who are blind, deaf, in wheelchairs, or with service dogs? How could you care for them?
2. What general and unique items should be on a trustee checklist?
3. Are you aware of members who currently have a hard time seeing or hearing during worship or Bible class? What could be done to address these issues?

Action Items

1. Walk around your church property inside and out with "visitor eyes." Work with your trustees and congregational leaders to address issues of concern.
2. Thank the Lord for the blessing of visitors, new members, and especially new Christians.
3. Schedule annual training sessions for elders, ushers,

and other servants of the congregation. Try a Saturday and provide breakfast and lunch. Consider using *Pastors and Elders: Caring for the Church and One Another* by Timothy J. Mech (St. Louis: Concordia, 2012).

4. Study why the LCMS teaches and practices closed Communion. Understand that this may be an emotional or controversial issue for some, but one where we must follow God's Word. Work toward better understanding and faithful practices consistent with sister congregations.

Jesus said: "For the poor you always have with you . . ." (John 12:8)

A caring pastor left a Latin American mission post to accept a call to serve a congregation in an American city. He prayed that St. Peter's Lutheran would welcome its Hispanic neighbors. After all, the church sign had room to say *Iglesia Luterana de San Pedro*.

The pastor faced resistance to reaching out to the neighborhood. "They're all Roman Catholic anyway, Pastor," he was sometimes told. He grew frustrated because of common ignorance of the fact that nearly half of the Hispanics in town were actually Pentecostal. How would his congregation respond to a sermon on the Good Samaritan (Luke 10:32–37)?

Who is *your* neighbor? We are given to care for the Christians the Lord Himself has gathered to our congregations. We dare not cast a blind eye on the communities—the people— that live nearby.

I dearly love the following prayer found inside the front cover of *LSB*:

> Lord God, bless Your Word wherever it is proclaimed. Make it a word of power and peace to convert those not yet Your own and to confirm those who have come to saving faith. May Your Word pass from the

ear to the heart, from the heart to the lip, and from the lip to the life that, as You have promised, Your Word may achieve the purpose for which You send it; through Jesus Christ, my Lord. Amen.

Witnessing

For all the baptized, witnessing Christ is supposed to be part of our way of life. We are to share our greatest gift, Jesus Christ, with anyone God allows us to meet.

Yes, it can be intimidating. Surprisingly, it gets easier as you do it more often. You will get rejections (or sometimes hear silence). Don't take such responses personally. They are not really rejecting you, but Christ's invitation. Your witness could change lives for eternity. Pray for the Holy Spirit to do His work of conversion where and when He so wills.

There are two types of witnessing:

1. You can tell about Jesus Christ yourself.
2. You can invite someone to Bible class and to church.

As a baptized, catechized Christian, you are equipped to do both! Church services and Bible classes are witnessing opportunities because both Law and Gospel are presented! In addition, Christians have been given two tasks:

1. Gospel outreach (caring for our neighbor's eternal needs: telling the Good News about Jesus)
2. Human care (caring for our neighbor's physical needs in this life: shelter, food, clothing, etc.)

Congregations that care for their communities do both Gospel outreach and human care. Both are important.

Caring for people's physical needs (human care) could get them curious about why you're helping. Then you can share Jesus. In that case, human care provides an opportunity for Gospel outreach. Often we hear of a fellow Christian in physical need. In that case, Gospel outreach leads to an opportunity for human care.

None of us *feels* perfectly equipped to witness. (This is yet another example of why we shouldn't trust our feelings.) None of us witnesses perfectly.

We witness by the power of the Holy Spirit, as stated in Acts 1:8: "You will be My witnesses . . . to the end of the earth." Peter states it this way in 1 Peter 3:15: "But in your hearts honor Christ the Lord as holy, always being prepared to make a defense to anyone who asks you for a reason for the hope that is in you; yet do it with gentleness and respect."

Jesus never says, "You should be salt and light" or "You could be salt and light" or "You might be salt and light." Nope. Instead He says, "You are the salt of the earth. . . . You are the light of the world" (Matthew 5:13–14). Christians have been given to "shake and shine."

The Lord has already prepared you for this important work. It doesn't have to be drudgery. It is actually an honor to be included in work that introduces people to Jesus! What a privilege to help prepare people for eternal life in Christ Jesus!

Keep It Simple: What Do You Believe as a Christian?

Remember all of that memory work in catechism class? It has a very practical use when someone asks you what you believe. Confess the Apostles' Creed!

The Apostles' Creed gives us a concise and faithful summary of all of Scripture we can share. We pray it at worship (both personally and corporately) to confess what we believe. We use it in catechesis to teach what we believe. Evangelism—witnessing—is teaching the faith once delivered to the saints. Much emphasis regarding Matthew 28:18–20 is placed on Holy Baptism, and rightly so. Baptizing and teaching together are what makes disciples.

We have been called to go and faithfully tell. It's not our job to convert or argue. We are not responsible for the results. It is the Spirit who converts people to Christ. That should take the pressure off. In addition, some very short Bible verses give us the opportunity to clearly confess and properly distinguish God's Law and Gospel.

> For there is no distinction: for all have sinned and fall short of the glory of God, and are justified by His grace as a gift, through the redemption that is in Christ Jesus. (Romans 3:22–24)

> For the wages of sin is death, but the free gift of God is eternal life in Christ Jesus our Lord. (Romans 6:23)

These and countless passages of Scripture are ready-made for you to memorize in order to care for others.

Enduring Witness, Enduring Mercy, Enduring Gifts

Of all the blessings we receive in this life, only a few blessings endure to eternal life:

God's love in Christ

God's Word (which endures forever)

God's people baptized into Christ
(recipients of forgiveness, life, and salvation)

The other gifts we have been given in this life are given for God's purposes, for His use, and not merely our own. We are to make use of them as His stewards, both in care of our families and in His work, that is, caring for anyone in physical or spiritual need. We always need to remember that we're dealing with people, not projects. God will bless us with good courage as we let Christ shine.

The current LCMS emphasis for the church uses the terms "Witness" and "Mercy." Both are done with the goal of "Life Together" in Christ. This ties in with the fact that congregations that care for their communities do both Gospel outreach and human care, often on the same occasion. In Mark 2:1–12, Jesus healed a paralytic and forgave his sins. Those gathered "were all amazed and glorified God, saying, 'We never saw anything like this!' " (v. 12).

Pray for eyes to see opportunities to help those in need in your community.

Getting Started with Human Care

Begin by studying everything meant by "daily bread." Luther's catechism questions are particularly helpful.

> *What is meant by daily bread?* Daily bread includes everything that has to do with the support and needs of the body, such as food, drink, clothing, shoes, house, home, land, animals, money, goods, a devout husband or wife, devout children, devout workers, devout and faithful rulers, good government, good weather, peace, health, self-control, good reputation, good friends, faithful neighbors, and the like. (Small Catechism, Fourth Petition)

Consider downloading and reading *Theology for Mercy* from LCMS World Relief and Human Care. That document can help frame a discussion of why we do what we do as Lutherans and how to do it with both discernment and compassion.

You could learn who is in your community through a demographic study. Getting out in your community can tell you things that statistics on paper simply cannot. Is your community a home to people new to America? Are there large numbers of undocumented immigrants? What languages are spoken? What ethnic groups were among the founding citizens of your city or neighborhood? How do they celebrate their heritage?

You have a great opportunity to witness and provide human care if there is a military base in your community. We're blessed to have a VA hospital and many veterans in our community.

As for something that affects everyone, make sure you know your city's major industries and employers. How do your actively working members earn their income? What is your local economy like compared to your state, region, and the nation as a whole? Ask questions like these so that you know what cares and concerns your community faces.

When People Show Up at Our Door: Social Assistance Tips and Cautions

Everybody seems to have a story of how they got to you and where they need to be. Be considerate and listen to as much as you can.

Keep gift cards on hand instead of cash for use when distributing funds to help families or individuals in need. Have a variety available for local restaurants, gas stations, and trusted businesses. Avoid abuse and misuse of limited funds by planning ahead.

Appoint specific people—apart from lay church office staff—who will talk with transients. When offering aid to nonmembers in the community, don't give cash. Cash can be easily misused on addictions. When choosing to provide aid, pay for gas, food, or lodging directly. These congregational almsgivers can then work with the person or persons in need to begin to build a relationship. Pray with and for them. Tell them about Christ and why you are helping them.

Communities could organize to pool resources for people "just passing through." A small city in our state did exactly that. After passing a basic police background check, travelers in need were given a voucher for one night's stay at a clean and safe motel, a hot meal at a local restaurant nearby, and either a tank of gas or a bus ticket to get them further toward their destination.

Pray for those you have already helped. Pray that they may be found on the narrow road of Christ Jesus leading to eternal life. Pray that they may safely reach their destination because of other friendly and generous Christians down the road. Pray for yourself for discernment and wisdom in unexpected circumstances.

One Sunday morning upon arriving early at church, I found a large man sleeping on the stoop of our door. I introduced myself. He told me his name and that he was blind and had other health issues. He said he was on his way across the country and that an ER nurse left him out on our doorstep a couple hours after midnight. I didn't believe the last part of his story. His accent and the team on his ball cap didn't fit his narrative. And I knew our hospital's policies better than he did.

I tried to warm him up in the parish hall with coffee. Someone had treated him to supper, but he couldn't keep it down. His wrist still displayed a hospital tag and evidence he was treated for dehydration. Did I mention he was an intimidatingly large man? A dear lady who makes coffee for

Bible class with her husband arrived as our visitor's story began falling apart. She greeted him, unaware of my growing concerns. Finally an elder arrived. He worked to find a way for the man to get closer to his destination. Another elder talked with the man while I quickly prepared to be ready to serve our congregation. That second elder followed his gut and called the police, asking for a background check on the man by name. Sure enough, he was blind, but he had been harassing congregations, human-care agencies, and assorted individuals all over town for the last three days. I kept praying that he would get the help he needed all the while, even after the patrol car arrived. This man needed help, yet we were unable to give him the help he needed.

How Should Help Be Distributed?

There will come a time when you will have done all you can do as an individual and a congregation. We are to care for others, but there is a limit to the hours in the day and the money we have to use. Limited funds and time need to be distributed with care for the sake of those truly needy. Those who distribute funds need to be accountable to your congregation and those donors who provide alms for this reason.

I encourage a healthy dose of skepticism when listening to stories you are told. Put the best construction on everything, but remember that only God's Word is 100-percent reliable. Don't be afraid to check up on details before giving aid. If someone calls us on the phone, we also ask that they refrain from calling every church in town. The experience gained in helping others has taught us to ask more questions.

"Will it do some good?" is a basic question we ask ourselves. There's little sense in pouring in good money after bad. If a person is six months behind on rent and your entire human care budget for the year can't cover one month's rent, there may be a more productive way to help than pouring money down a black hole. We found ways to help someone stay one night in a motel but were reluctant to put someone up for a week or a month.

We once helped a family out with a week's rent at a motel because the husband and father had just begun work at a convenience store—or so he said. When we couldn't help for another week, he was offended. A year later, his family was featured on the front page of our local newspaper as the beneficiary of a free month's stay at that same motel courtesy of another congregation. No mention was made in the article of the long-term nature of their abuse of the system. Several motels in our community got a bad reputation for asking semi-long-term residents like this family to call every church in the phone book to foot the bill for their stays. I now often see this man and his family about town, usually with a full cart in one of the discount stores and spending a lot of time near the electronics department. I never did see him work a day at that convenience store.

Don't feel guilted into helping someone holding a cardboard sign near a stop sign of a store parking lot. Offer to buy the person a meal. He or she may even accept your offer, because the need may be real. Don't be surprised, though, if the person turns you down or asks for cash instead. Some people "make their living" off the generosity of motorists passing by all day and then go back to their homes.

"Where will help come from next?" is a related question. Helping someone make it until payday is one thing. Providing for large financial needs for a long time is something else. Sometimes a compassionate "no" can help someone face up to reality sooner rather than later. Also ask, "Is this a high-priority need?" We've had to turn down requests to help people pay for their cable TV service. We have honored requests to keep heat and the lights on.

"What is your home congregation?" is our first question to someone who calls us on the phone or walks in the door. Only rarely do we hear, "I'm a Lutheran. I went to St. John's by the gas station back home." We've even had local people call us because we *weren't* their home congregation. They were simply too embarrassed or too proud to ask their own fellowship for help. A follow-up question, "Did you used to have a home congregation?" may also yield an answer that can lead to a referral.

Why ask, "Do you have a home congregation"? With so many people in real need and so many others scamming the system, this question may lead to a pastor back home willing to vouch for the person to the pastor of a sister congregation in your area.

We have found many people to help by asking these

questions. We helped one young man with gas to get to work whose only connection to us was attending Sunday School decades ago. I pray that we will see him and others like him again. Nevertheless, follow-up is difficult, even when the people you help are locals.

Scams

Not everyone who asks your congregation for help is truly in need. I pray you can learn from our experiences, including our mistakes.

One of the first requests we received for some gas after I arrived at my current congregation was by a woman who had a convincing story. We could fill her tank that day and did. She came back two months later and was upset when we turned her down. A week after this, a man came by asking for gas. He seemed nervous, but his story was well-practiced. It turned out to be her partner/husband/boyfriend. We turned him down when we saw her sitting in the backseat of his car.

Others made phone calls to the churches and charities in town. They would say something like, "Yeah, hi. Mr. Smith over at St. Jude's Anglican referred me to you." The jig was up when we got a fake referral from someone who didn't exist who supposedly worked for a charity that does not do referrals.

So what happens if you are scammed? Did you sin, or did the other party? The Seventh Commandment teaches, "You shall not steal. *What does this mean?* We should fear and love God so that we do not take our neighbor's money or possessions, or get them in any dishonest way, but help him to improve and protect his possessions and income" (Small Catechism).

Your congregation fears and loves God so that you are generous to those in need. Your goal is to serve your Lord by serving someone who needs to care for himself or herself. Your intent is to keep the Seventh Commandment. The scammer is the one who is at fault. His or her intent was to break the Seventh Commandment.

A scam is a chance for a caring congregation to learn something and do better next time. Even if someone does take advantage of your caring congregation's generosity, do not be discouraged from being generous in the future. Remember Jesus' words in Matthew 10:8: "You received without paying; give without pay."

Funding Generosity

The most natural way to fund social assistance is through your budget. The amount will vary depending on your congregation's size and location.

Pastors, encourage members to be generous from the pulpit. Have fund-raisers to support human care outreach through your congregation. Benevolent groups may be able to provide funds to supplement your social assistance budget.

What has your congregation actually spent on human

care needs in the past? Such research may help your budget be more realistic and substantive enough for the task at hand. Carefully steward funds with the whole year in mind. Special situations may require appeals for additional funds.

Very few congregations are equipped to provide a full soup kitchen, food bank, thrift store, showers, short-term housing, or a free clinic. These are areas where we can find ways to work with other caring people in our communities, including a council on social agencies, a ministerial association, or other local options. You may find opportunities to sit with lonely shut-ins or volunteer at your hospital in a family waiting room. Look for ways to make use of the interests and vocations of those in your congregation to serve your congregation and community. Focus on things you actually can do.

Martha and Mary

> Now as they went on their way, Jesus entered a village. And a woman named Martha welcomed Him into her house. And she had a sister called Mary, who sat at the Lord's feet and listened to His teaching. But Martha was distracted with much serving. And she went up to Him and said, "Lord, do You not care that my sister has left me to serve alone? Tell her then to help me." But the Lord answered her, "Martha, Martha, you are anxious and troubled about many things, but one thing is necessary. Mary has chosen the good portion, which will not be taken away from her." (Luke 10:38–42)

Whatever the mission project, whether it is Gospel outreach or human care, doing the work of the Lord requires a sacrifice of time, talent, or treasure. Human care serves the primary mission, Gospel outreach. It does little good to purchase vehicles in a mission field where there is no one there to do Word and Sacrament ministry. Human care is a good and salutary thing, especially as we serve our neighbors around the world, but we need to remember that it is always done in service to the Gospel message: Christ crucified and risen for the forgiveness of sins!

Encourage your congregation to be generous to the national church body through your district.

Christians have been called by the Lord to preserve His pure doctrine, tell the Good News about Jesus, and care for those in need. None of these responsibilities may be neglected.

Consider your own failures in these areas. Confess your sins and hear Christ say, "The Son of Man came not to be served but to serve, and to give His life as a ransom for many" (Mark 10:45). You are part of that many. Live in His forgiveness, and serve others in the freedom of the Gospel.

Caring for the community around your congregation is very rewarding. Being able to meet the needs of those who truly need help gives great joy. It can also help you better understand what it means "to receive our daily bread with thanksgiving" (Small Catechism, Fourth Petition).

Key Points

- The two kinds of mission are Gospel outreach and human care. Doing one often blesses you with the opportunity to do the other for the same person.

- Be generous and prudent when sharing social assistance. Give gift cards, not cash. Ask if the person in need has a home congregation. Discourage the desperate and needy from calling every church in town.

- Recognize the need for Gospel outreach and human care locally, regionally, nationally, and globally.

Discussion Questions

1. Read Luke 10:38–42 again, and ponder how it applies to your service to your Lord and congregation and what projects and activities you could choose for the new year. Which roles are "Martha" work? Which could be called "Mary" work? Which type, according to Luke 10:42, is primary? Why?

2. What human care opportunities are in your community? Do you have a crisis pregnancy center? Can you donate to an organization that has an aid fund for those needing help with rent, utilities, or medical bills? Can you send books to a seminary overseas? Can you make the time to visit the hospitalized, imprisoned, lonely, or those in care facilities?

3. Write a paragraph describing the people of the neighborhood around your church . What steps can you take to include them in congregational life and, hopefully, membership?
4. What gaps are there with regard to social assistance in your community? How could your congregation help meet those needs?

Action Steps

1. Study the "Theology for Mercy" developed by LCMS World Relief and Human Care (http://www.lcms.org/Document.fdoc?src=lcm&id=735) and follow that up with a group Bible class reading of *Christ Have Mercy: How to Put Your Faith in Action* by Matthew Harrison.
2. Pray for eyes to see opportunities for your congregation to care for your surrounding community.
3. Encourage your congregation to increase non-designated giving to the Synod through your district.
4. As you care for those of the household of faith, learn more about the life and work of the original St. Nicholas. Consider making his feast day, December 6, a day to remember the less fortunate just as he did.
5. Are you retired? Do you live very near to your church? Consider making yourself available to help your pastor (and church office secretary) with visitors with human care needs during weekday hours.

"And when did we see You a stranger and welcome You, or naked and clothe You? And when did we see You sick or in prison and visit You?" And the King will answer them, "Truly, I say to you, as you did it to one of the least of these My brothers, you did it to Me." (Matthew 25:38–40)

According to our vocations, we Christians witness and provide mercy for the sake of our life together. A very special way a congregation can become more caring is by intentionally examining how it cares for its pastor or pastors and its other professional church workers.

Former Wyoming District President, Rev. Dr. Ron Garwood, wrote, "It has been said that every pastor ought to have six weeks of vacation each year, because if he is a real good pastor, he deserves it; and if he is not a very good pastor, his congregation deserves it."

We are given to care for one another. Pastors care for their congregations, especially through visitation. Congregations are given to care for their pastors and their families. Let me explain how the pastors and congregations in our district do just that on a larger scale.

The Wyoming District doesn't have circuit counselors. Instead, they are called circuit visitors (CVs). In the 1990s, convention action returned us to the older term used in the Preface to Luther's Small Catechism, the Saxon Visitation Articles, and the German-era history of the LCMS.

Synod does count our CVs as circuit counselors, and in the age of "Witness, Mercy, and Life Together" as a churchly emphasis for the LCMS, returning to this historic terminology would remind pastors, congregations, and servants of both in the district and the Synod of the circuit visitor's (circuit counselor's) role in ecclesiastical supervision. Once every three years, our district president, with the assistance of circuit visitors and district vice presidents, makes an official visit to every congregation in the district.

This caring work is carried out to ensure that pastors are taking care of their congregations' theological and spiritual needs and that congregations are taking care of their pastors physically and spiritually.

Why Care for Pastors?

Many Lutheran commentators in previous generations used Jesus' parable of the sheep and the goats (Matthew 25:31–46) to teach Christians to care for those who filled the Ofce of the Holy Ministry and not merely everybody in need. Focus on the word *brothers* in verse 40:

This chapter focuses primarily on the care a congregation ought to provide for pastors and their families. Keep in mind that many of these reasons and obligations apply also to the other professional church workers who bless your congregation. The authority and responsibilities of these other positions flow from the pastoral office itself, and those who hold them need the full care and support of the congregation as well.

> And the King will answer them, "Truly, I say to you, as you did it to one of the least of these My brothers, you did it to Me."

According to what Bible translators tell me, the Greek word translated as "brothers" here could be translated as "brothers or sisters." While I believe that is true in many contexts, it refers to the Office of the Public Ministry here and also in some other specific places in the New Testament.

Matthew 28:10 is another example: "Then Jesus said to them, 'Do not be afraid; go and tell My brothers to go to Galilee, and there they will see Me.'" Consider also the specificity of John 20:16–17: "Jesus said to her, 'Do not cling to Me, for I have not yet ascended to the Father; but go to My brothers and say to them, "I am ascending to My Father and your Father, to My God and your God."'"

There are many passages where the Lord teaches us to care for the poor. We examined some of them in chapter 3. Consider the whole of the persecution borne by Jesus' twelve disciples in the Book of Acts and in Early Church history, and there is ample evidence of those very disciples being hungry, thirsty, sick, and imprisoned for the sake of their Gospel ministry.

Beyond this, congregations care for pastors and their families for many reasons. Let's consider a few mentioned in Scripture.

> Let the one who is taught the word share all good things with the one who teaches. (Galatians 6:6)

> We ask you, brothers, to respect those who labor among you and are over you in the Lord and admonish you, and to esteem them very highly in love because of their work. Be at peace among yourselves. (1 Thessalonians 5:12–13)
>
> In the same way, the Lord commanded that those who proclaim the gospel should get their living by the gospel. (1 Corinthians 9:14)

Let's get very practical and specific. How should pastors be compensated for proclaiming the Gospel?

Reimbursing Ministry Expenses

In our day, pastors usually need motorized transportation to visit their people. Some congregations own a vehicle that they register, insure, service, and keep fueled. The pastor is expected to use the church's car for church business in such cases.

It appears to be more common for the pastor to have his own vehicle. He keeps mileage records for congregation business, submits those records monthly, and receives the current IRS mileage reimbursement rate. The pastor has the freedom to choose his own wheels. Mileage reimbursement is the same for a pickup or a compact car, so economic considerations on fuel efficiency will be left up to him.

It's not worth skimping here. A pastor should be encouraged to visit his flock. Unrealistic budgets can subtly discourage that work.

Other reimbursable expenses may include business meals and entertainment, vestments, professional gifts, books, journals, office supplies, and so on, according to our current district guidelines. Possible disputes can be avoided by having a process in place where permission for expenditures is approved in advance and supported with receipts after the purchase.

Health Care
—Physical, Spiritual, and Emotional

Healthy workers serve their congregations better. Care for your pastor's health so he can better care for your spiritual health.

The obvious first steps include providing him with quality health care, disability, and retirement plans. This doesn't mean you have to necessarily get the most expensive plan available; it does mean you should do your research. Find out what other churches offer, talk to your pastor (or area pastors if you are calling a new pastor) about his family's health needs, and find a plan that suits both your budget and your conscience. There are areas where some skimping may be okay, but your pastor's health is not one of them. Help him put worry aside by taking care of both present and future needs.

In caring for your pastor's health, ask whether your pastor takes his days off. I could ask that question in another way: Does your congregation give your pastor the opportunity to use his days off, reserving non-life-and-death issues for his work days? Does he have freedom to reschedule days off in order to fit his family's busy schedule? Does he get a make-up day when life-and-death emergencies deprive him of his usual day off?

I learned early on as a pastor to take Friday as my day off. Mondays were too busy with "Pastor, I forgot to tell you about . . ." messages and visits about unfinished items from Sunday's handshake line or pre-Bible class rush. I may also have a portion of Saturday, too, if there are no meetings, classes, weddings, or LWML events. I love having Friday off because I am usually better rested and ready for Sunday morning, my workday with the highest expectations.

Encourage your pastor to take his days off. This is not only for his sake, but for his family's sake (even if unmarried, he still has a mother, father, and siblings) and, ultimately, for the congregation's sake. Encourage your pastor's wife to protect his days off from anything work-related, even from social situations with members.

If your pastor has hobbies, encourage them. Help him find ways to unwind. Feel free to invite him to learn about your hobbies or local leisure opportunities, yet give him the freedom to be himself.

Continuing education time; time serving the circuit, the district, or the Synod; and military reserve and jury duty do not count as vacation time! District or synodical conventions or monthly circuit conferences don't count as days off. Too often they tend to be much more work than rest!

Congregations can show care for their pastors and nurture their emotional health by giving extra time off, over and above district guidelines. Christmas, Easter, Thanksgiving, birthdays, and anniversaries away from family are hard on church workers and their families. Don't forget how difficult it may be for their parents and siblings. Consider celebrating October as Pastor (and family) Appreciation Month to show your congregation cares.

Salary and Benefits

What if every congregation everywhere paid pastors with similar experience and expertise the same? I've told congregations that salary and benefits should not have to be a consideration for a pastor when considering a call. Wouldn't it be nice if pastors could just focus on the ministry opportunities of both congregations compared to his own strengths and weaknesses?

The 2010 convention of the LCMS encouraged congregations to follow the guidelines of their district in providing for their pastors and their families. In our district, the guidelines used to be compiled by our Commission on Mission Services because they were intended as mandatory for congregations receiving district assistance. After adoption by the District Board of Directors, they were commended to all congregations as minimum guidelines. Unfortunately, they were not and largely are not seen as minimum guidelines for self-supporting congregations.

After five declined calls were received by a congregation I served in vacancy, they were finally convinced of the importance of paying a pastor according to his experience in the district guidelines. Offering a pastor a call to their congregation with a $10,000 pay cut compared to where he was currently serving was *not* a good idea.

Salary considerations can also send specific messages to a pastor with regard to his service at a given congregation. A pay cut may be a signal to the pastor that they want him to move on. Keeping a pastor at the same salary year after year after year is not encouraging to him, to say the least. Even during hard economic times, a modest raise, or at least a cost-of-living increase, can be a great encouragement to all who live in the parsonage.

It is best to follow district guidelines. They often show recommended salaries based on years of experience, special added duties (such as serving a multi-point congregation, working as headmaster of the congregation's school, etc.). These provide a great reference point for compensation for all church workers by comparing apples to apples: you can compare what your pastor or teachers are making to what the district says is the proper base pay rate for these well-trained and committed individuals. It's true that people don't choose church work to get wealthy, but that's not an excuse to take advantage of their desire to serve without complaint.

I'm not trying to beat a dead horse, but if district compensation guidelines are required for subsidized congregations, why are they so often ignored by self-supporting congregations? Our district recommends them to congregations as mere *minimum* guidelines. The freedom of the Gospel allows them to show appreciation over and above these minimum recommendations for their servants of the Word.

Awkward Moments and a Church Worker's Best Advocates

It is a touchy thing to ask for a raise in the secular world of employment. It can be even more so in the congregation, for everyone at the budget adoption meeting of the voters assembly know exactly what the church workers make.

While district presidents and circuit visitors (counselors) can and should be good advocates for pay and benefits consistent with district-recommended minimums, the reality is that some congregations may decrease mission dollars giving to districts in order to give those raises. As a result of this reality, some district officials may find it to be counterproductive to encourage congregations to follow their own guidelines.

The best advocates for care of the pastor (and other church workers) are not pastors or their wives, but caring congregation members themselves.

The board of elders is usually given the task of specifically caring for the pastor—just as the school board is typically charged with caring for the teachers. This is an important yet delicate task. I have tried to limit discussion of my own salary and benefits to one annual mention of the availability of the revised district guidelines with my elders. Then, I recuse myself from further discussion of these budget line items at the subsequent elders, council, and voters meetings. I do ask that the head elder let me know how things went once the budget meeting is over via a phone call to the parsonage.

Our LCMS pastors are among the best-trained clergy in the world, truly theologians in the pulpit and biblically informed, passionate caregivers for our congregations and communities. No, pastors are not "professionals" in the same way we think of medical doctors and lawyers, yet they have equivalent years of education and often similar debt. Consider blessing a new church worker or pastor with a debt retirement gift. Life in the parsonage can be financially tight at any time, and especially during a pastor's first years in the parish.

I once heard how indigenous missionaries in a new mission field receive their living from the Gospel as servants of the Gospel and have a salary comparable to the people in the community that they serve. Their idea may inspire your caring congregation.

If ten families tithed, the pastor would then get a salary proportionate to that community. The same thing would happen with twenty families giving 5 percent.

Consider asking ten actively working members (not retired) what they make. Keep the information confidential or anonymous. Add the salaries together and divide by ten. Or get a wider representation of income from twenty actively working members. Add them together and divide by twenty. I'm convinced if you try out this little experiment, you'll find that the district guidelines for your pastor's salary aren't so bad after all.

The Parsonage

If your congregation has a parsonage, how is it maintained and when was it built? How many bedrooms does it have and what is storage like? Is there modern heating and cooling? Who does the maintenance? Is lawn care provided?

Are basic utilities provided as part of your congregation's investment in a parsonage?

When considering a call to another congregation, a district president actually *warned* a pastor about the parsonage. It seemed everyone knew that the house was deficient and little had been done (except for paint and insurance-paid repairs after the basement flooded) to improve the situation.

Please care for the church's parsonage as if it were your own home. I can tell you from experience that it is difficult to be in the position of a permanent "renter."

I can encourage you as a reader by accounts of how congregations better met the housing needs of their pastors' families through their parsonages. One congregation, taking note of the sad condition of their parsonage during an extended vacancy, acted on an opportunity to buy the fully furnished home of the community's late bank president. They made a significant dent in their new loan when they held an auction to sell most of the unneeded furnishings. Selling the prior parsonage paid off most of the rest of the loan. A second congregation added on to their 1950s parsonage in anticipation of receiving a new pastor with a larger family. The new master bedroom with bath, additional upstairs bedroom and bathroom, and finished basement, along with a garage with room for two vehicles, was greatly appreciated by the new pastor and his family. A third congregation sold the old parsonage and purchased one in great condition just a block away from their new church. It took hard work, frank discussions, persistent prayer, and a year of meetings to get consensus, but it showed they and their pastor could work together as a team.

Pastoral Manliness

Brother pastors, please change your own light bulbs. Keep your home picked up and organized. Roll your trash bin down to the street yourself. Help with trustee projects that you propose to improve and maintain the parsonage. Help with maintenance and projects around the church property too. When they redo the sprinkler system or when a dead tree is removed from the lawn, lend a hand. Habitat for Humanity calls such work "sweat equity." You may not be able to help in every situation, nor should you, but some participation shows your congregation that you care and are invested with them as a team. And it helps the men in the congregation respect you as a man as well as God's preacher in their midst.

I've personally painted two parsonages. I thank the Lord that my father is a retired carpenter and contractor. Knowing how to shingle, put up drywall, and work hard have been great blessings to me as a pastor living in parsonages. One of my first trustees taught me how to safely replace home electrical outlets (receptacles) and light switches. We all have different skills and experiences, but there's always something you can contribute or learn.

Mrs. Pastor and Family

My wife was once asked the difference between "the wife of a pastor" and a "pastor's wife." The difference, it usually seems, is one of expectations: a "pastor's wife" is sometimes expected to do it all.

An American president's wife may get the ceremonial, unpaid role of first lady, but don't assume that the wife of your pastor will automatically join the quilters' guild, be a soloist in your choir, play the organ every other Sunday, teach Sunday School, be considered as the new church secretary, and be a Martha-Stewart-level cook and hostess for congregational events. Do you have the same unrealistic expectations of every new female member? No? Then why reserve them for the wife of your pastor?

Instead, encourage the wife of your pastor to get to know the congregation, trying different activities before officially joining. Give her the freedom and support to serve according to her gifts and talents. Especially encourage her in her primary vocations of wife to her husband and mother to their children. Recognize and appreciate that in these vocations she serves not only her husband but the congregation, as she is your pastor's primary support behind the scenes.

Be friendly to the wife of your pastor. Mere pleasantries don't cut it when someone needs true friendship in a new place, especially a place far from her parents and siblings.

Pray for her and their children. Be especially encouraging (and the opposite of nosy) if they haven't been blessed with children. Don't assume that your pastor is ignorant about adoption. Love them as the unique individuals and family they already are in the Lord's service.

Realistic Expectations and Life Together

How much are you asking your pastor to do? Does your congregation have truly realistic expectations of what he has been given to do? Have you thought about how to care for and encourage him when there aren't enough hours in the day to get done all that his call documents ask of him?

I've learned that there is a big difference between faithfully and conscientiously serving a congregation of two hundred baptized members and a congregation of eight hundred baptized members with a school.

If you find that your congregation is facing some challenges in providing your pastor and church workers with a healthy work environment, you may want to check out *Holding Up the Prophet's Hand: Supporting Church Workers* (CPH, 2012)

Reviewing all the thoughts in this chapter, ask if the congregation is allowing for adequate compensation and time off. Is your pastor's time off actually restful, or is it often unnecessarily interrupted? Work together with your pastor to address any shortfalls in these areas.

We are given to love one another. That means putting up with one another for the long haul. Issues in congregations can be long-term, deep-seated, and downright difficult. There may be a temptation toward bitterness and resentment among the people of God.

Care for one another as Christ cared and still cares for you. Help your pastor serve with joy. Give double honor to those who serve well. Focus on helping him feel appreciated so that he and his family would be happy to stay in that little corner of paradise on earth forever. Sometimes, budget arguments and member attitudes degrade the congregation/

pastor relationship over time. Work proactively to prevent this.

Don't forget to help your pastor help you. One way to do this is by letting him know when you or another congregation member is in the hospital. Privacy laws prevent the hospital or its workers from notifying him. He can't go if he doesn't know! Let him know anytime you need a visit.

The small things matter too. Honor the pastor's study as a private place he can prepare for catechesis and worship, as well as do pastoral care and counseling. Be forgiving to the church office when there is an unfortunate overlooked typographical error. Only Jesus is perfect, not you or your pastor. We imperfect people are given each other to work with. Care for your undershepherd of Christ, our Good Shepherd, for the sake of the Gospel.

Key Points

- Care for your pastor, his family, and other church workers for the sake of the Gospel.
- Avoid pastoral family stereotypes and encourage his family members to serve in their gifted areas, prioritizing the wife supporting her husband behind the scenes.
- By working with your pastor to care for him, you are also caring for your congregation.
- Notify your pastor if you or another congregation member is in need of a pastoral visit. He can't go if he doesn't know.

Discussion Questions

1. When does your LCMS district update and distribute church worker salary guidelines? Where is this information kept at your church?
2. Is the congregation allowing for adequate compensation and time off? Is your pastor's time off actually restful, or is it continually interrupted?
3. Do the constitution and bylaws of your church describe how and when the budget is prepared and approved? Does this process usually happen on time? What can you do to help it happen on time?
4. How large should a congregation get before an additional pastor is needed? Is the congregation open to a vicar (intern pastor-in-training)? Would it be more appropriate to start a daughter mission congregation in the area? Are there possible preaching stations that could become mission starts?

Action Items

1. Follow your district's guidelines for minimum salary, benefits, time off, retirement, housing, and health care. Care for your pastor because he cares for you. If you say you follow district guidelines on a call document to a new pastor or other church worker, don't allow your congregation to find an excuse to not continue to do so.
2. Pay extra attention to parsonage maintenance so the

pastor can focus on the ministry of the Gospel.

3. Help your elders and pastor find "first aid" emergency pastoral care coverage for his days off, vacation time, and other times when he is away.

4. Encourage your district to resume, begin, or continue triennial visitations of every congregation, pastor, church worker, and school by the district president, vice presidents, and circuit counselors.

And let us not grow weary of doing good,
for in due season we will reap, if we do not give up.
So then, as we have opportunity, let us do good
to everyone, and especially to those who are
of the household of faith. (Galatians 6:9–10)

After twenty-eight years of paying on a mortgage, a family had foreclosure proceedings begun against them. We sent out an appeal to help this family while trying to keep them anonymous. Donors came forward. With the Lord's help, we were able to keep that family in their home.

Months later, a similar situation occurred with a young couple in over their head on a home far too large for them. Congregation and family assistance made it to the bank to avoid foreclosure with an hour to spare. This couple has since downsized their home to better meet their needs, had a child, and has received at least a year's worth of financial counseling.

We Christians are given to care for our own. At times in this chapter, I will speak specifically to pastors. Lay leaders and congregation members are invited to overhear what I have to say to your pastors. In the same way, pastors are invited to listen in to my advice to the Christians at large in our Lutheran congregations.

Visitation Is Our Heritage

At its beginning, the LCMS saw the importance of care for one another through visitation. The Synod president himself visited every congregation and pastor each year. As the Lord blessed the LCMS with further growth, the Synod divided into districts so that each district president could visit every pastor and congregation in his district every one, two, or three years. Eventually, the Synod saw wisdom in appointing circuit visitors (circuit counselors) to assist the district president and the Synod president in assisting with these now triennial visitations.

The apostolic model of Acts and the New Testament Epistles comes from our Lord Himself.

> What do you think? If a man has a hundred sheep, and one of them has gone astray, does he not leave the ninety-nine on the mountains and go in search of the one that went astray? And if he finds it, truly, I say to you, he rejoices over it more than over the ninety-nine that never went astray. So it is not the will of My Father who is in heaven that one of these little ones should perish. (Matthew 18:12–14)

Jesus also said: "I am the good shepherd. I know My own and My own know Me, just as the Father knows Me and I know the Father; and I lay down My life for the sheep" (John 10:14–15).

Pastoral Care

One particular six-letter word means the same thing in Latin, German, and English: *Pastor*.

A pastor is a shepherd, an undershepherd of the Good Shepherd, Jesus Christ. Shepherds take care of sheep, of Christians in Christian congregations. All of this should be obvious and clear. Unfortunately, it often isn't. The lost sheep, lost coin, and lost son parables of Luke 15 remind us of how we should rejoice in the return of those who are lost.

Pastoral care is a balance between study of the Word and care based upon that Word of God. I therefore encourage you to "Do your visits." What does this mean? Well, we should fear and love God (and the people entrusted to our care) to be available in times of emergency when called. When in doubt, go. If you can't physically be there, call a brother pastor or one of your elders. Prison, hospital, nursing home, and shut-in visits should be done regularly and consistently. There is nothing like a one-on-one visit to get to know a person.

Our seminary classes on pastoral care encouraged us to do initial every-member visits to help us get to know our people in their natural habitat. Why stop doing them?

People change. Our families grow and change. Kids grow up. Children are born, are baptized, begin Sunday School, may attend the congregation's Christian Day School, begin catechism classes, are confirmed, participate in youth group, graduate from high school, and often leave home for college, technical training, the military, or to otherwise begin their adult lives.

Make home visits before a Baptism or wedding, before young people begin formal catechism instruction, and as an invitation to begin (or resume) Sunday School, especially after graduating from cradle roll. Consider visits to high school seniors at the beginning and end of senior year. Be sure to follow up on visitors to church services or Vacation Bible School.

Premarital catechesis including what the Bible teaches on holy matrimony is essential. Include sessions on the Small Catechism, financial matters, sexuality, and communication, including mutual confession and forgiveness. Follow-up visits can be helpful on the first anniversary after a wedding. Couples have marital crises, lose loved ones, and struggle to live as Christians in a fallen world.

Prioritize a visit to mourners a month, six months, or a year after a funeral. Remember the first wedding anniversary or birthday of a deceased spouse after a funeral.

Shepherds take care of sheep. This is true for those "keeping watch over their flock by night" (Luke 2:8) and for those of us who care for souls purchased and won by the blood of the Lamb of God, who takes away the sin of the world.

Visits are not only for shut-ins. They never have been. They help a pastor get to know his people and the people get to know their pastor. This is where they learn and see that he cares. New pastors are often encouraged to love their people. This is but one more way to do so as a caring congregation.

Dear pastors, fulfill your call and regularly visit your people. Dear congregations, be open to a visit from your pastor. Help him avoid the awkwardness of the appearance of "inviting himself over."

What was once considered normal pastoral care in our life together has, in some times and places, become extraordinary. "Uh, oh! Pastor wants to come over. What did we do wrong?"

Emergencies will disrupt the most comprehensive and well-planned visitation schedule. Even if it takes years, keep the goal of visitation.

The *LSB Pastoral Care Companion* is one more tool you should consider in addition to your Communion set, Bible, hymnal, and catechism in your pastoral care toolkit.

A pastor visits his people. Brother pastors, spend mornings (and occasional afternoons) in your study doing paperwork and computer work, but get out of our study and into the homes of your community at least every other day.

Elders

Elders in some congregations may be used to only assisting with Sunday morning. I encourage pastors and elders to train together so they may do visits together. Pastors can model how to do such visits as they visit the households of each elder. A pastor can invite an elder on an appropriate home visit to show how one is done.

The number of elders should be proportional to the size of a congregation. This may depend on geographical and distance considerations. A congregation's membership could be

To clarify and strengthen the roles and relationships between pastor and elders, check out *Pastors and Elders: Caring for the Church and One Another* (CPH 2012).

divided into elder responsibility areas based on the alphabetical order of a membership directory, geography, or some other way.

Another way to show care for a congregation is an intentional, short-term every-member visit conducted by the pastor, elders, and other winsome volunteers, possibly from stewardship, evangelism, and assimilation boards or committees. I recommend focusing visits to two or three months.

On such every member visit initiatives, I do not recommend asking for money for a building project, debt retirement, or other cause. Simply extol the Lord's gifts at Divine Service in Word and Sacrament. Say, "God has good gifts for you at ___ Lutheran Church." Such a visit would show that you care about them. The goal is inreach. The motive is to provide better pastoral care and congregational support to those who are already members of the congregation.

Jesus teaches about reconciliation in the oft-quoted portion of Matthew 18. Yes, this is the passage upon which the godly practice of excommunication is based. The goal remains reconciliation, yet our Lord is such a Lord that He allows Himself to be rejected: "If your brother sins against you, go and tell him his fault, between you and him alone. If he listens to you, you have gained your brother" (v. 15). What is the goal of this verse? Reconciliation. Is there to be any gossip, complaining to others, or generalized badmouthing of the person who did you wrong? No.

Reconciliation is the goal, as in verse 16: "But if he does not listen, take one or two others along with you, that every charge may be established by the evidence of two or three witnesses." This verse still remains the pattern in a court of law. The goal is that two or three Christians can work to reconcile with that same original brother or sister who sinned against you. Reconciliation is the goal!

Read verse 17: "If he refuses to listen to them, tell it to the church. And if he refuses to listen even to the church, let him be to you as a Gentile and a tax collector."

Whenever someone brings up the idea of "cleaning the membership rolls" by some blanket standard, I say, "No" automatically, and then tactfully and patiently explain our true goal of reconciliation. While denouncing unrepentant sin is important, making membership decisions about groups of members simply because they haven't been in attendancein a while is irresponsible and not the mark of Christian love. The Office of the Keys must be wielded carefully and precisely.

A final comment on visitation: if there is a need to do a visitation of the congregation's membership to appeal for funds or pledges, I suggest the alternative of an active member visit, focused only on folks who have attended services at least twice in the last six months. Be upfront about the visit's purpose. Be specific about what the funds would be spent on.

Caring through Christian Education

A child's first teachers are his or her parents. Even small children can learn the Lord's Prayer, the Creed, and other basics of the faith. As a congregation, do everything you can to encourage parents to actively teach their children the Christian faith at home. Then you can build on this with what you teach at church.

Christians taught the faith to children long before there was Sunday School. Congregations can best care for children during Sunday School by teaching God's Word. Realistic art of Bible people helps reinforce the fact that our stories are actual, historical accounts. You may even wish to wean yourself off of the use of the term *story*, since so many tales of the story genre took place "once upon a time."

Teach children hymns, liturgical songs, catechism parts, and Bible verses that reinforce the main lesson. Teach children songs that are fun, yet put a stronger emphasis on songs that they can grow into rather than grow out of. Playtime and crafts should be purposefully related to Bible teaching and not mere filler.

Vacation Bible School is a wonderful opportunity for a focused teaching of God's Word while having fun. It takes extensive time to prepare for a VBS. I recommend songs and hymns for openings, music time, and closings that can be used beyond VBS week. Look for hymns that fit your VBS theme yet could also be incorporated into fall and winter Sunday services to engage VBS attendees longer-term.

Youth confirmation class should focus on Luther's catechisms as a guide to the whole Bible. I am blessed to teach Luther's Large Catechism to eighth graders after they have been grounded for two years in Luther's Small Catechism. My wife recalls two or more years of study of the Old and New Testaments before she began her years of official confirmation instruction.

In all that you teach, give the children in your church more than the bare minimum of faith instruction. You want them to be learners for life—eternal life.

Lutheran Day Schools

Show care for the parents and children of your congregation by starting or supporting a Lutheran school. Heed Christ's call to follow what God's Word says, to practice what we preach. He calls for biblically informed, passionate, and faith-filled teaching and practice at home, church, and school. Christian education has always been important to Lutheran Christians.

Lutherans such as Johann Sturm, Philip Melanchthon, and Martin Luther revived classical education in their day, founding a proper education on Christ and His Gospel. They also advocated for education for all, including girls and peasants, and a free public Christian education paid for by the state, especially if the head of state was a Christian prince.

Why did the Saxon Lutherans leave Germany in the 1830s? Most of us are familiar with the problems with unionism and syncretism in Germany. Recent scholarship shows that they were more concerned with the sad state of German schools than even the theological problems of the state church. They were troubled by the fact that what was taught in the state schools contradicted the Christian faith that was taught at home and at church.

When the LCMS was first founded in 1847, there were sixteen original congregations and fourteen original schools. From the 1870s through the early 1900s there were more schools than congregations in our church body.

Christian education is important to Lutherans. It all begins with the Fourth Commandment. Imagine having a school at your congregation where the worldview and content taught is consistent with the Scriptures and the Lutheran Confessions and with what is taught in church and at home.

Teaching Adults

Catechesis for new adult members should be in-depth, tailored to the previous religious backgrounds of the participants, and give participants familiarity with the Bible, Small Catechism, and hymnal. I have used various formats over the years. My favorite framework is to use the Gospel according to Matthew to teach the faith. After all, isn't that why it was written?

In the first sessions, I give a brief tour of the Small Catechism's Six Chief Parts, the *Lutheran Service Book*, and the Bible. Our main focus is reading Matthew 1–2 word for word, with volunteer readers taking turns in a safe environment.

Matthew 1 shows immediate connections to the Old Testament and familiar names to most people from Sunday School. Matthew 2 is a brief celebration of Christmas. I emphasize the miracle of the incarnation and direct the class to study the Second Article of the Apostles' Creed and Luther's meaning. In addition to opening and closing devotions and plenty of time for the members-to-be to ask questions, we would continue reading Matthew.

Week 2 would mean reading Matthew 3–4 and covering Holy Baptism from the Small Catechism. Week 3 would expose them to Jesus' Sermon on the Mount in Matthew 5–7 and Luther's Small Catechism's explanations of the Lord's Prayer and the Ten Commandments.

I'm sure you can see the pattern we develop, along with an environment of trust and a positive, personal pastoral-care relationship.

When I served a congregation that was essentially a mission post in a town that was two-thirds Mormon, I used special catechesis resources to address the challenges of that religious and cultural context. We care best for those Christians entrusted by the Lord to our congregations and our pastoral care by teaching them God's Word substantively, comprehensively, and unapologetically.

Recent national surveys of the "formerly unchurched" have confirmed what I have always expected. They're not turned off by denominational labels, such as "Lutheran." Musical style preference is near the bottom of the things they were looking for. What they really wanted to find was somebody, somewhere, who actually and truly believed what they publically taught and have historically confessed to be true. That is who we are!

Allow me to state another tidbit of uncommon sense: Lutherans are on the cutting edge. It is a wonderful time to be a biblically knowledgeable, theologically capable, liturgically equipped, hymnologically rich, personally engaged, and Christ-centered Christian church. And that is exactly what Lutherans are! Taking the time to teach Bible substance is never wasted time.

A Shut-in "Watch List"

For me, one of the biggest differences between serving a typical congregation of two hundred baptized members and one of over eight hundred baptized members has been the number of shut-ins, those dear saints of God who can no longer physically attend Divine Service on Sunday morning.

My previous habit was to visit each and every shut-in member twice a month. That hasn't been possible at my current call, where I have between sixty and eighty shut-ins or seasonal shut-ins and potential shut-ins on my "Watch List." I feel blessed to see each and every one of them at Divine Service, at their home, nursing home room, or in a medical emergency or surgery situation once every six to eight weeks.

I take the visitation part of my call as pastor exceptionally seriously. Even when my afternoon of planned shut-in or other visits is interrupted by a valid congregational (or school) emergency, I still feel guilty about not making those previously planned visits right away.

How often should shut-ins be visited? That depends on your congregation's size, number of people to visit, and the size of your pastoral staff. Our congregation recognizes that our pastoral care needs are more than one called servant of the Word can handle. We're working on how best to care for our own baptized members. When "shut-ins" can make extended shopping trips and nonmedical appointments, I strongly and lovingly encourage them to come on Sunday morning like other able-bodied saints of the congregation.

I encourage visits to shut-ins by members of the congregation beyond the pastor, elders, and official leaders. This builds more connections between members and a sense of community beyond just a pastoral care relationship with one particular pastor. Lay visitors won't distribute the Sacrament of course, but they can deliver bulletins and *Portals of Prayer* in true Christian love and care, with a hearty "we've missed you."

Congregational Infrastructure

Individuals in a given congregation often don't realize how unfriendly or uncaring they are perceived by others. Even institutions can encourage or discourage visitors and new members.

Church boards and committees should regularly review the congregation's constitution, bylaws, and other governing documents to ensure that they are being followed. If they're not being adhered to, ask why not. Do the behaviors need to be changed or the rules? If the rules are changed, make them more closely follow what the congregation is actually doing or is capable of doing. For "the Sabbath was made for man, not man for the Sabbath" (Mark 2:27–28).

Publications may become just "one more thing to read," instead of the essential sources of information that they are intended to be. Consider digital versions alongside print and bulk-rate mailed versions. Don't assume that people read the whole newsletter or the whole bulletin. Having a well-used monthly calendar and weekly announcement sheets may be more effective for small congregations than a bulky, unread congregational newsletter.

A caring congregation should celebrate photos of its family. Do a congregational membership directory with photos at least every five years, especially after a new pastor comes on board. Or consider an up-to-date congregational family photo wall. If you decide to do either project, work with someone who will take submitted photos. We've recently done a hybrid of these two ideas. We self-produced a photo directory and have a new "update" photo wall where we can post photos of new members, also including Baptisms, confirmations, weddings, and special congregational events like Vacation Bible School.

Families also celebrate their past. Consider posting photos of confirmation classes, significant historical photos from the whole history of your congregation, and good photos of every pastor who has been called to serve your congregation.

This is another good way for new members to get to know your congregation, both past and present. Share these photos and a copy of your directory with them so they can put names and faces together.

It's especially important to welcome all new members who have joined your congregation through youth or adult confirmation, Baptism, affirmation of faith, or transfer from a sister congregation. Liturgically, we welcome them with a rite from the *LSB Agenda*, a handshake, and a place to stand or kneel next to us at the Lord's Table. But is that all?

You could have an official welcome basket delivered by a member of the LWML. You could also have a new member dinner annually on Reformation Sunday or just before quarterly voters meetings. Friendship cannot be forced, yet introductions can always be made based on common neighborhoods, hobbies and interests, career fields, ages of children, and among those joining your congregation at the same time. Some churches assign people to specifically welcome and assist new members. Consider finding "sponsors" (like at a Baptism) for new families to the congregation.

Whatever else you do, encourage current members to be friendly and to personally introduce themselves to anyone new.

Life Together

Over the years, I have observed many ways congregations and pastors have encouraged and cared for one another. This section will give you a sampling.

The men of my current congregation are manly Christian men. They have been active for generations in Bible study with one another on days other than Sunday. One group meets at 6 a.m. at a local diner every Monday. Another group has a larger men's Bible breakfast at the church at 7 a.m. on the first Saturday of each month. They have paint sample cans they use for their "mites," which are spent on projects to benet our congregation and school.

At my first congregation, I inherited a home Bible study evening called Breadbreakers. It sounded similar, yet different from the "triangle suppers" of my vicarage year where three neighborhood families from the congregation regularly got together for an evening meal in their homes. It also had elements of an organized potluck or carry-in dinner. Here's how they worked. One family would volunteer to host Breadbreakers in their home each month and provide the main dish. Others who wanted to attend would call that month's host and ask what side dishes they should bring. As pastor, I would prepare a fresh Bible study. Not surprisingly, we studied "bread" in the Bible for the whole first year. The evening would begin with a thought-provoking icebreaker section that would lead into the evening's Bible study topic. We would then have our main meal together, followed by the main portion of the Bible study. Dessert was served after the closing prayer. We avoided Breadbreakers turning into a clique or "church within the church" by regularly inviting new participants personally and having two of these dinners at the church where we randomly mixed up the groups (if there were more participants than could fit in a typical home).

The quilters of our congregation make hundreds of mission quilts each year. We always seem to have new ladies join our group that works most Wednesday mornings and then enjoys lunch together, often with our schoolchildren in our church basement. Our basement serves us well as a space for Sunday School opening, our school cafeteria, a school and congregational library of thirty bookcases, and of course, our quilters paradise. Sewing machines, worktables, and fabric are well organized. We get along well, especially when each group that uses the basement respects the other groups that use the same space.

Paid print, radio, or Internet advertising, church signs, and community concerts can create awareness about your congregation, namely, that it exists, but they do not create a caring congregation. There is nothing like personal invitations to church. More people join our congregations because they were invited to church than for any other reason. If someone you know already knows you well and knows that you care about them, they might just show up! Better yet, invite them to church and offer to pick them up on Sunday, or at least offer to meet them in the church parking lot so you can walk in with them.

As a congregation, work to develop opportunities for people to begin and strengthen relationships. Consider offering marriage enrichment classes. Brainstorm different ways you can support the youth, young adults, and widows of your congregation. Ask what other groups could use special help. While your church's central focus should always be Word and Sacrament ministry, find ways to provide care in other ways as well.

Shake and Shine as Salt and Light

> You are the salt of the earth, but if salt has lost its taste, how shall its saltiness be restored? It is no longer good for anything except to be thrown out and trampled under people's feet. You are the light of the world. A city set on a hill cannot be hidden. Nor do people light a lamp and put it under a basket, but on a stand, and it gives light to all in the house. In the same way, let your light shine before others, so that they may see your good works and give glory to your Father who is in heaven. (Matthew 5:13–16)

Caring for one another best begins with repentance and confession of how we have failed to love, care, and serve in the past according to our vocations.

I hate to sound trite or too much like a TV shrink, but "acknowledging the fact that you aren't caring is the first step." That is Law—heavy Law. Yes, we will fail. We have already failed. That does not exempt us from trying.

Still, to declare only the Law is incomplete Christian proclamation. Walther reminded us that "the Gospel must predominate."[1] The sin of not caring for others is also a sin forgiven by Christ Jesus. What we do in our care for others in Jesus' name flows from God's work in us by the Holy Spirit and His Word of Gospel (Galatians 2:19–21). Remember: Caring is not an end in itself.

---

1. C. F. W. Walther, *Law & Gospel: How to Read and Apply the Bible* (St. Louis: Concordia, 2010), 456.

The primary way we care for congregations as Christians is by delivering the forgiveness of sins from God in Christ. And the Lord delivers His gifts, Word and Sacrament, at the Divine Service. Article V of our Augsburg Confession shows who we are as Lutherans and why we do what we do:

> So that we may obtain this faith, the ministry of teaching the Gospel and administering the Sacraments was instituted. Through the Word and Sacraments, as through instruments, the Holy Spirit is given [John 20:22]. He works faith, when and where it pleases God [John 3:8], in those who hear the good news that God justifies those who believe that they are received into grace for Christ's sake. This happens not through our own merits, but for Christ's sake. Our churches condemn the Anabaptists and others who think that through their own preparations and works the Holy Spirit comes to them without the external Word.

Only the Lord creates true fellowship among Christians. His Divine Service is where heaven and earth intersect, a preview of the great multitude of all tribes and peoples and languages in white robes that John saw (Revelation 7:9–10).

Your Vocations

Review your vocations in life in the light of God's Word. Consider the fourfold framework of priorities on the next few pages. I developed them as a young pastor through some interesting circumstances.

A caring couple had lived across the street from a Lutheran parsonage for thirty years. They knew our congregation's office secretary because she also did the bulletins for their non-Lutheran congregation. They told her they were frustrated by a congregation and church body that had decided to believe what was politically correct and then reinterpreted Bible verses to prop up their new teachings. Instead, this couple wanted a congregation that said, "This is what the Bible says. Therefore, that is what we believe and teach." They soon visited us and joined.

Not long after they became Lutherans, the husband was laid off his middle-management job only eighteen months before he was eligible for early retirement. He spent his time both looking for work and finishing the honey-do list of household projects his wife had for him. During this time, he lost fifty pounds and was able to stop taking at least two medications under doctor's orders. Still, he was frustrated to be out of work.

One day he was offered not one but three jobs. The first offer came from their daughter in Florida. "Mom and dad, you can live in our pool house if you walk our dog twice a day." "Nice offer," they answered, "but we're not ready to retire just yet." The second offer came from a company in California. He would do nearly the same kind of job he had before, but with a significant raise. The third offer came from an outfit in Missouri, close to both St. Louis and the original Saxon Lutheran colony that birthed the LCMS. "Pastor," they asked, "what should we do?"

After much thought, prayer, and study, I came up with a list of personal priorities together that applied the Ten Commandments in what you will read below. "Where will we go to church?" was their major concern. Our congregation hated to lose them, but we rejoice that they became very involved in their new congregation in Missouri.

First: Baptized Child of God

We are each given to receive the Lord's gifts. Commandments 1, 2, and 3 speak to this (see Exodus 20:1–11, Luther's Small Catechism on Commandments 1–3, and especially the First Commandment). What the Bible teaches about Holy Baptism is clear about who we are in Christ, notably whose we are.

In Matthew 22:33–40, Jesus helps us better understand the Commandments of God as love toward Him and care for our neighbors. That passage also gives fresh perspective on your second-most important vocation.

Second: Member of a family—son or daughter, single person, husband or wife, father or mother

We are given care for the family the Lord has placed us in, keep our marriage vows, and raise children as Christians. Carefully study the Fourth Commandment and the Sixth Commandment as well as Ephesians 5:21–6:4.

Third: Worker

As workers we are given to provide for the Lord's work and priorities as well as the family God has given to us. This is how we keep the Fifth Commandment as well as heed 1 Timothy 5:8; 1 Chronicles 29:11; and 1 John 3:16–18.

Fourth and Last: Everything Else (Leisure, hobbies, community involvement, sports, spectator sports, and even serving at church)

We are given to keep vocational priorities 1–3 first. Beware of burnout among servants of the church (both clergy and laity) when priority number 4 takes precedence over priority number 1. Consider Mary's and Martha's priorities in Luke 10:38–42. Not all church activities are equal.

Luther's Small Catechism directs us to love the Lord and care for our neighbor according to our vocations. (See also the Table of Duties). We are also to confess our sins according to our vocations:

> *Which [sins] are these?* Consider your place in life according to the Ten Commandments: Are you a father, mother, son, daughter, husband, wife, or worker. Have you been disobedient, unfaithful, or lazy. Have you been hot-tempered, rude, or quarrelsome? Have you hurt someone by your words or deeds? Have you stolen, been negligent, wasted anything, or done any harm? (Confession)

All of our Bible study, all of our care about what happens on Sunday morning, every witness of the Gospel of Christ, every act of human-care ministry, every way pastors care for congregations and congregations care for their pastors goes back to who Jesus is and how He cared for and still cares for us!

Key Points

- Pastor and congregation members care for one another best by visiting members in their homes, especially in times of need. Inreach is just as important as outreach. Provide Gospel care to every member.
- Be intentional about catechizing and assimilating new members.
- Friendship cannot be forced, but introductions can be made to connect people with one another.
- Part of caring for others is setting godly vocational priorities for yourself.

Discussion Questions

1. When was the last time a pastor paid you a visit at home or in an emergency situation? When was the last time you invited your congregation's pastor over to your home?
2. In the past, how did your church nurture a sense of family or community? Could these traditions be updated for today?
3. When does your pastor hold new member classes? Ask him if you could attend a refresher course.

Action Items

1. Ensure that your congregation has adequate pastoral care and elder coverage for its size and geographical

reach. Equip every elder with the books *Visitation* and *Pastors and Elders: Caring for the Church and One Another* by Timothy J. Mech.

2. Consider an every-member visit of your congregation. Set a focused time to accomplish all visits. Train winsome volunteers well. Don't ask for money. Say, "God has good gifts for you in Christ at _____ Lutheran Church." Our motive is inreach and providing pastoral care, not "cleaning the rolls."

3. When a fund-raiser is needed to expand pastoral care, build, or retire debt, consider an active member visit, focusing only on members who have been in church recently. Be up front that you are asking for financial support for a specific purpose.

4. Offer a marriage workshop at your church.

5. Update your congregation's photo membership directory or photo wall, or develop one for the very first time.

> Humble yourselves, therefore, under the mighty hand of God so that at the proper time He may exalt you, casting all your anxieties on Him, because He cares for you. (1 Peter 5:6–7)

I learned to truly love and be comforted by 1 Peter 5:6–7 because of evening chapel during my seminary years and particularly because of a service we prayed on Thursdays called Compline, Prayer at the Close of the Day. Lutheranized from the form Luther himself used as a monk, it seemed like a perfect way to remind ourselves of the comfort of the Gospel in the midst of a stressful life. Lutheran spirituality means a fresh start of forgiveness in our vocations because of Christ every new day.

Turn to the full musical version of the service on pages 253–59 in *Lutheran Service Book*, or begin with the more concise outline form on page 298.

After opening verses from Psalm 92, those assembled confess their sins and absolve one another. A common psalm used for Compline is Psalm 4. I love faith's condence in a caring Lord expressed in the nal verse: "In peace I will both lie down and sleep; for You alone, O Lord, make me dwell in safety."

Following a hymn, there are brief Gospel-filled readings, including 1 Peter 5:6–9:

CONCLUSION

> Humble yourselves, therefore, under the mighty hand of God so that at the proper time He may exalt you, casting all your anxieties on Him, because He cares for you. Be sober-minded; be watchful. Your adversary the devil prowls around like a roaring lion, seeking someone to devour. Resist him, firm in your faith, knowing that the same kinds of suffering are being experienced by your brotherhood throughout the world.

After silence for reflection, threefold repetition convinces us of the truth of Psalm 31:5: "Into Your hands [O Lord] I commend my spirit" (*LSB*, pp. 255–256).

Another hymn is followed by more psalm versicles and collects like this: "O Lord, support us all the day long of this troubled life, until the shadows lengthen and the evening comes and the busy world is hushed, the fever of life is over, and our work is done. Then, Lord, in Your mercy grant us a safe lodging and a holy rest and peace at the last; through Jesus Christ, our Lord." My personal "Amen" to this prayer is having it framed and on my desk to comfort me every day I care for the people of God.

The Lord's Prayer leads in to singing the Nunc Dimittis (*LSB*, pp. 258–259) using a Gregorian chant form. It also includes this antiphon, a psalm-like introduction and conclusion to the Luke 2:29–32 canticle of Simeon: "Guide us waking, O Lord, and guard us sleeping that awake we may watch with Christ and asleep we may rest in peace." This is how I wish the Nunc Dimittis to be prayed at my own funeral.

I was taught that Compline helps us to view our bed each night as our deathbed so that when we nally lie on our deathbed, ready to meet Jesus face-to-face, it will be no more frightening than falling asleep at night. When I helped a dear aunt plan her own funeral, she told me, "I may fear dying, but I need not fear death." She knew that she would fall asleep in Jesus and awake in the heavenly mansion He prepared for her. She knew her Lord's care for her. She cared for me by sharing her confidence in His care for her.

> Lord, now You let Your servant go in peace; Your word has been fulfilled. My own eyes have seen the salvation which You have prepared in the sight of ev'ry people: a light to reveal You to the nations and the glory of Your people Israel. Glory be to the Father and to the Son and to the Holy Spirit; as it was in the beginning, is now, and will be forever. Amen.

> Guide us waking, O Lord, and guard us sleeping that awake we may watch with Christ and asleep we may rest in peace.

As you endeavor by faith, in prayer, and grounded in God's Word to help make your congregation a more caring church, may "the almighty and merciful Lord, the Father, the Son, and the Holy Spirit, bless you and keep you. Amen" (*LSB*, p. 259).

www.ingramcontent.com/pod-product-compliance
Lightning Source LLC
Chambersburg PA
CBHW071312040426
42444CB00009B/1982